D0810865

Published in the USA by:
S&J Publishing
www.thehqlprotocol.com

Printed in the United States of America

ISBN: 978-0-9863636-0-3 (paperback)
ISBN: 978-0-9863636-1-0 (ebook)

Depression
Post partum depression
Feeling sad or close to tears
Crying easily
Suicidal thoughts
Anxiety, nervousness, or panic attacks
Excessive worry or fixed attention
Low thyroid
Low energy
Chronic fatigue
Exhaustion
Shortness of breath
Heart races or palpitates
Dizzy spells
High blood pressure
Ringing in the ears
Pressure in head, eyes, forehead
Pressure in sinuses
Tight muscles in head, neck, shoulders
Headaches or migraines
Trouble falling asleep
Trouble staying asleep
Toss and turn at night
Waking too early
Excessive dreaming
Nightmares
Short term memory loss
Foggy thinking
Poor concentration
Feeling hotter than others in the room
Hot flashes
Night sweats
Irritability to rage
PMS
Mood swings
Heavy periods with flooding, clotting
Painful cramps

Irregular periods
Monthly cycle shorter than 28 days
Spotting between periods
Miscarriages
Breast lumps or tumors
Cervical thickening
Endometriosis
Uterine fibroids
Polycystic ovaries
Ovarian cysts
Tender or painful breasts
Decreasing periods
Skipping periods
No periods
Vaginal dryness or irritation
Painful intercourse
Sugar cravings, especially chocolate
Midriff weight gain
Water retention
Facial hair growth
Hair growth in unwanted places
Scalp hair loss
Decreasing sexual desire or libido
Decreased sensitivity in erogenous zones
Pimple or acne on the face or body
Changes in eyesight
Bone loss
Lowered immune function
Sinus infections
Vaginal infections
Bladder infections
Low blood pressure
Irregular pap smears
Breast cancer
Cervical cancer
Uterine cancer
Vaginal cancer
Vulval cancer

Any of This Sound Like You?

Read this book and find out what you can do about it...

Introduction

 My name is Sindi Holmlund and I've been in the alternative health field for over 40 years. I formulate and manufacture chemical free health and beauty products, I'm an herbalist, a researcher, a writer, I own a clinical diagnostic laboratory and a compounding pharmacy, and I **was** a menopausal woman.

At age 27 I developed chronic vaginal infections, cystic ovaries, and my breasts were swollen and sore all the time. About age 32 I started experiencing extreme fatigue, long, heavy periods with spotting all month, rapid weight gain, acne, my breasts became even more sore, low blood sugar, sugar cravings (especially chocolate) and an inability to conceive.

These symptoms continued for about seven years. Then some new ones joined in, and life became a nightmare for me and my husband. I either cried or screamed at the drop of a hat, everything my husband did was wrong and I continually threatened to divorce him, I started having horrible dizzy spells, my periods became light and I started skipping them, my skin aged practically overnight, my vision started changing, I grew a fatty tumor on my shoulder the size of my palm, my hair started falling out, I gained 35 pounds, the muscle tissue on my body disintegrated, I couldn't sleep, my memory started taking vacations, I couldn't concentrate, the sugar cravings doubled, I would wake up several times in the night because I was too hot and throw off my covers, only to wake a while later to put them back on because I was now too cool, and my breasts became so painful that often, the weight of them (and I was small breasted) brought tears to my eyes when I got out of bed in the morning.

Because the second set of symptoms was different from the first, and had started seven years later, I had no idea they were related. I also had no idea what was causing them. So for 6 years I went from doctor to doctor, spending thousands of dollars, trying to find out what was wrong with me, but NONE of them had the answer. Oh they said they did, and sold me hundreds of dollars' worth of supplements that did *absolutely nothing!* It wasn't until around age 44 when I started having mild hot flashes that I realized my hormones were changing, but I still didn't know that *all* my symptoms were because of those changes. The problem was, no one else knew it back then either.

I'm knowledgeable about many things but hormones was a subject in which I was *completely* ignorant, So I went to the library (no internet back then) and checked out every book I could find about hormonal changes. All they had were books about menopause, but that didn't fit me because I was still having periods, and they only listed hot flashes and night sweats as accompanying symptoms. I took all the books back and went to the medical book store at a local college and bought books about anatomy and physiology, endocrinology (hormones) and Tabor's medical dictionary. It was a *grueling* learning curve because I had to learn so many technical and medical words, but 6 months later I fully understood that all my symptoms were caused by hormone decline, and that decline had started **at the end of puberty!**

What I also understood was that the subjects of how your body works and hormone decline are two things that you cannot afford to be ignorant about, because ignorance in either subject can cost you your **life!**

In studying these subjects, I learned a lot of information I wished I had known when I was 18. If someone had told me back then, what I'm going to tell you now, I would never have suffered the way I did for so long. So in the hopes that I can spare you what I went through, I'm writing this booklet. I want to share what I know with as many women as possible so *they* can recognize when hormone changes begin and know what to do about them.

The first thing you need to know is how your reproductive cycle works, so I'm going to explain that with loads of pictures.

OKAY, HERE WE GO...

Let me define two key terms that I'm going to use in this book...'Pre-Menopause' and 'Menopause'. Menopause (Definition: *menopause - meno = menses [menstruation] + pause = to stop or cease*) is that time in a woman's life when she has not had a menstrual cycle for 12 months. At that time, if she has no more periods, she is considered menopausal. Pre-menopause (Definition: *pre-menopause - the time between the end of puberty and when a woman stops menstruating*). During those years, reproductive hormones are declining and it's that decline that causes the symptoms of pre-menopause.

IN THE BEGINING...

You are born with about 400,000 egg follicles in your ovaries. These follicles, or sacs, contain microscopic, immature eggs.

(Definition: *follicle* - any small sac or cavity.)
(Definition: *ovaries* - either of a pair of female glands producing eggs and sex hormones.)

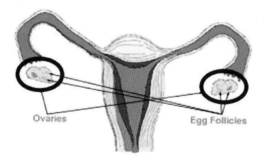

Ovaries   Egg Follicles

Day one of your menstrual cycle is the day you *start* your period. Your menstrual cycle is supposed to be 28 days long, but due to hormonal changes it can become longer or shorter. But in this publication, I'm talking about a 28 day cycle.

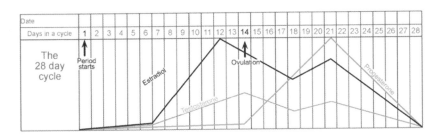

On day *one* of your cycle, the pituitary gland in your head begins to send increasing amounts of a hormone called 'Follicle Stimulating Hormone' (FSH) down to your ovaries. This hormone stimulates the ovaries to start maturing several hundred egg follicles.

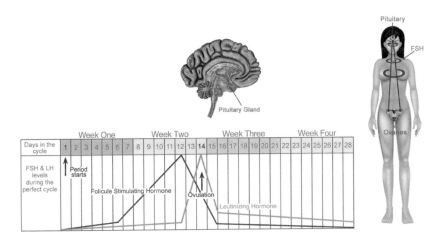

For the first 12 days, as the eggs mature, they release increasing amounts of estrogen, and a minute amount of progesterone.

(Definition: *estrogen* - estro = estrus = frenzy + gen = something produced. The period of sexual excitement, or 'heat', of female mammals. Estrogen is something that produces a sexual frenzy in mammals compelling them to have sexual intercourse to fertilize an egg and achieve pregnancy.)

(Definition: *progesterone* - pro = for + gesterone = gestation, pregnancy.)

5

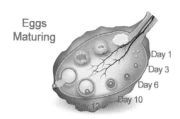

Eggs
Maturing

Day 1
Day 3
Day 6
Day 10

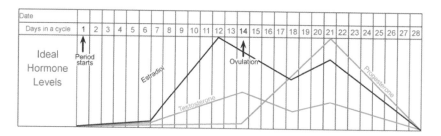

Date																												
Days in a cycle	1	2	3	4	5	6	7	8	9	10	11	12	13	14	15	16	17	18	19	20	21	22	23	24	25	26	27	28

Ideal Hormone Levels

Period starts

Estradiol

Ovulation

Testosterone

Progesterone

As your pituitary secretes increasing amounts of FSH, it causes your ovaries to release increasing amounts of estradiol and progesterone. A portion of those hormones is sent to back to your pituitary as a progress report. This is how it keeps track of how the monthly cycle is progressing. The correct amount of hormones tells the pituitary that egg production is on schedule for the next phase of the cycle.

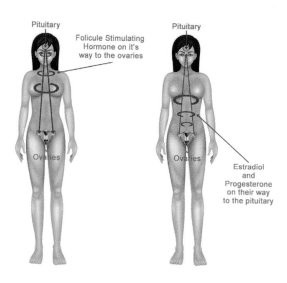

Pituitary

Folicule Stimulating Hormone on it's way to the ovaries

Ovaries

Pituitary

Ovaries

Estradiol and Progesterone on their way to the pituitary

There are three main estrogens, Estradiol, Estrone and Estriol, and they all do different jobs in your body. Estradiol is responsible for building the bloody lining of the uterus, retaining water, swelling the breasts and, in general, getting your body ready to receive, and implant, a fertilized egg into the uterus

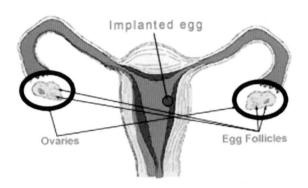

On day 12 of your cycle, estradiol peaks (see chart above) and the pituitary stops sending FSH to the ovaries. For the next two days the pituitary surges a second hormone called **Luteinizing Hormone** (LH), which triggers the release of one of the ripened eggs. That release takes place on day 14, and is called **OVULATION**.

(Definition: *Luteinizing* - to cause to turn yellow.
Lutein is the Latin word for 'yellow'.)

(Definition: *ovulation* - to discharge an egg from an ovary.)

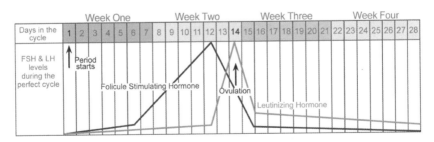

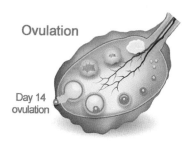

Ovulation

Day 14
ovulation

After ovulation, the sac that the egg was released from turns **yellow** and begins to release increasing amounts of progesterone during the third week of the cycle.

The rest of the maturing eggs die off and start to shrink. As they shrink, they release less and less estradiol, and its level starts to decrease. If the egg is not fertilized when it reaches your womb on day 21, both estradiol and progesterone plummet and the bloody lining is shed in what's known as menstruation.

(Definition: *menstruation* - to have a normal flow of blood from the uterus, about every four weeks.)

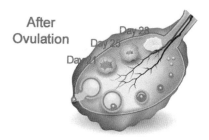

After
Ovulation

Day 28

Day 28

Day 21

The rest of the matured eggs die and start to shrink. As they shrink, they release less and less estradiol, and its level starts to decrease. If the egg is not fertilized when it reaches the womb on the 21th day, both estradiol and progesterone plummet and the bloody lining is shed in a process known as menstruation, and the whole cycle starts over again.

(Definition: *menstruation* - to have a normal flow of blood from the uterus, about every four weeks).

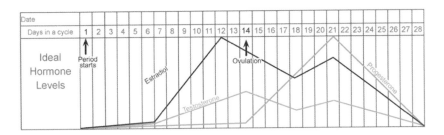

LATER IN LIFE...

This cycle goes on month after month, year after year, and causes the supply of eggs in your ovaries to decrease. That leads to less and less eggs maturing each cycle, and less and less estradiol being released into your blood. At some point there is not enough estradiol to cause the necessary peak on day 12 and signal ovulation. No ovulation means no progesterone the last two weeks of the cycle.

Even though there isn't enough estrogen to cause ovulation, there is still considerably more of it than progesterone. This causes a situation called **'estrogen dominance'** or **'unopposed estrogen'**. That means that estrogen is the **'dominant'** hormone and there is no progesterone to oppose it. And it's the *absence* of progesterone which causes the dominance of estrogen, which, in turn, causes the symptoms of **pre**-menopause.

Estrogen Dominance

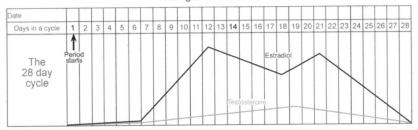

UNDERSTANDING ESTROGEN DOMINANCE

Most women don't actually understand what estrogen dominance is. They tell me they think it means that they're making too much estrogen, which it doesn't.

The chart below shows that in a normal cycle, your estradiol peaks on day 12, and it's that peak that signals ovulation. After ovulation you can see that your progesterone level rises steeply for the next 7 days.

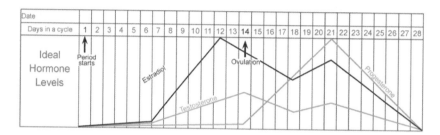

That's because it's produced by the 'hole' that's left in your ovary after the egg is released on day 14.

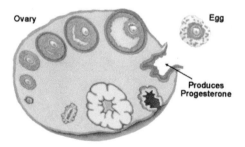

Like I said earlier, you're born with only so many eggs in your ovaries, and it's those eggs that produce your estradiol. Each month you use up hundreds of those eggs, causing your supply to decrease. As it decreases, so does the amount of estradiol secreted into your blood stream. At some point you will not have enough eggs to produce enough estradiol to signal ovulation, and if there's no ovulation, there's no progesterone the last 2 weeks of the cycle. From the chart below you can see that the estradiol is only about 5% low, but it's enough to cause a total absence in progesterone the last two weeks.

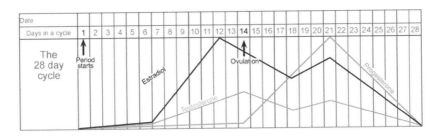

Estrogen dominance is not really an accurate name for this condition. It should have been called 'progesterone deficiency', because it's the missing progesterone that causes all the problems. The lack of ovulation causes the lack of progesterone, which causes too much of the available estradiol to enter your cells the last two weeks of your cycle.

Estradiol tells cells to divide and multiply, which is how tissue grows. One of the main tissues estradiol tells to grow is the lining of your uterus, and one of the main jobs of progesterone is to prevent about half the estradiol in the blood stream (the last two weeks of your cycle) from entering the uterine cells and over-building its lining. If all the available estrogen were allowed to enter your uterine cells the last two weeks of the cycle, it would double its lining.

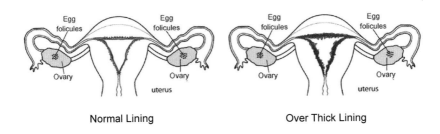

Normal Lining   Over Thick Lining

Estrogen dominance usually occurs somewhere between 30 and 40 years of age and can be recognized by changes in your menstrual flow; it becomes heavier than normal, clotty (they're not actually blood clots, their pieces of uterine tissue), can last longer than normal, can cause breakthrough bleeding, spotting after your period ends, more than one period in a 28 day cycle and heavier than unusual cramping.

Not only does exposure to all that estradiol over-build uterine tissue, it does the same to your breast, cervical and vulvar tissue. If progesterone is not there to stop all the available estradiol from reaching those tissues, it can easily cause uterine fibroids, cystic breasts, cystic ovaries, and uterine, ovarian, breasts, cervical and vulvar cancer.

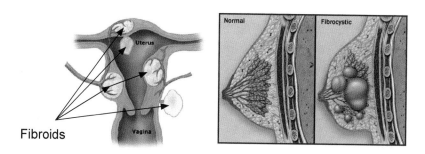

Progesterone is black and white. If you don't ovulate, you don't have any the second 2 weeks of your cycle...simple. But that's not the case with estradiol, it declines slowly, over a long period of time. At first you will just experience the symptoms caused by the missing progesterone, but sooner or later you will also experience symptoms of your estradiol getting too low, and the lower it goes, the more the symptoms increase.

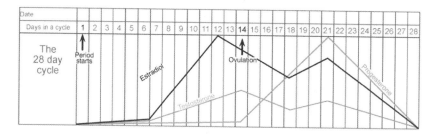

As your estradiol declines, your period will become more 'normal' again. As it continues to decline your period will start getting lighter, then your periods will begin to skip, and when it's extremely low, your period stops altogether. So if your periods were heavy and are now more "normal" again, they're getting lighter, you're skipping them, or no longer having them, you are not estrogen dominant.

Remember, the main characteristics of estrogen dominance are:

- Changes in the menstrual flow
- More than one period in a 28 day cycle
- Flooding
- Periods lasting longer than 7 days
- Very heavy flow
- Spotting between periods
- Heavier than usual cramping
- Breakthrough bleeding
- Expelling large amounts of uterine tissue

YOUR HORMONES DON'T START CHANGING AT 50

When I first started making and selling creams that contained progesterone, estradiol and DHEA, women between 30 and 45, who were still
menstruating, would tell me about a variety of symptoms they were experiencing. When I would mention the word hormones they would say
that it couldn't be that, because they were too young. So I would have to
spend about an hour explaining how it could be hormones. After which,
they put on some cream containing progesterone and in a few minutes
they would feel better. Then they understood that their symptoms were,
indeed, caused by declining hormones.

**(Definition: *symptom* - something which shows that something
else exists, indication, sign. Any condition accompanying a
disease and helping in its diagnosis)**

What women (and men) don't understand, because no one teaches
them, is that hormones don't start changing around 50 years of age,
they start changing around age 6. Prepuberty is from around 6-9 years
of age, and puberty starts about 9. During puberty, hormones skyrocket.
Puberty ends around 18-20 years of age and at its end, hormone levels
begin to decline. THAT'S IT! They go up, then they go down.

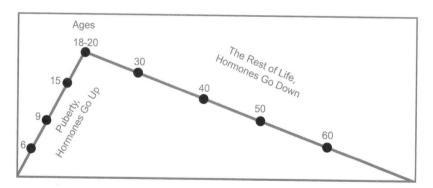

Estrogen alone performs over 400 functions in your body (and testosterone does the same thing in men). Therefore, as it declines and those
functions are greatly hindered, or just stop, and you begin to experience

symptoms. So, because hormone levels begin to decline around 18 years of age, it's easy for you to start experiencing symptoms by age 25-30. Experiencing symptoms of hormone decline before you stop having periods (menopause) is what has come to be known as pre-menopause.

There are at least 115 symptoms of hormone decline, but the one you're probably most familiar with is hot flashes. You may not even know you're having them when they first start, because they can be very mild, you just get a bit too warm from time to time. Heart palpitations can accompany hot flashes, but since you don't know this either, you can think there's something wrong with your heart, and end up spending a bunch of money only to find out it's just fine.

Hot flashes may be the most familiar symptom of hormone decline, but you probably don't understand why you're having them, so allow me to explain what they are, why they happen and why they can cause heart palpitations.

ABOUT HOT FLASHES

Throughout the month, your pituitary gland closely monitors estradiol and progesterone levels, because they tell it if the eggs are maturing on schedule. If they are not, evidenced by not enough progesterone and estradiol in the blood, your pituitary will dilate your blood vessels and surge Follicle Stimulating Hormone down to your ovaries in an attempt to raise production.

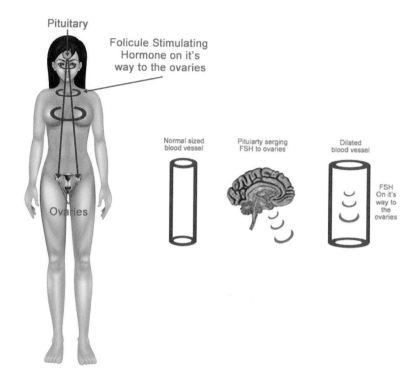

As blood vessels dilate, blood is driven closer to the surface of your skin, which causes it to become warmer and turn red. The redness is the characteristic 'flushing' known as a hot flash. If you were to look in a mirror during one, you could actually watch your chest, neck and face turn red.

This process causes more than just a warm or hot feeling and a red face. As your blood vessels open, your central nervous system has to speed-up. This can cause symptoms ranging from slight nervousness to an outright panic attack. Breathing also quickens and you may feel the need to take one or more deep breaths all of a sudden.

At the same time your heart sharply contracts and beats more rapidly to speed-up the flow of blood to your widened blood vessels. This can cause anything from a slight heart flutter or palpitations, to a sharp pain in the chest. If you're not familiar with this process, you could think you were having a heart attack.

As your heart rushes additional blood to your brain, your head can start to pound and you can become light headed, dizzy or in extreme cases, faint.

Sweating is the body's way of cooling itself down, so after a hot flash you may begin to sweat just a little, or to the point where you need to change your clothes.

Hot flashes that occur while you're sleeping are called night sweats. (I've don't understand why they need a different name). Night sweats can be so severe that you can wake up feeling you're unable to catch your breath and think you're having a heart attack. They can cause you to wake up and throw off your covers because you're too warm, fall back asleep and wake-up again a little later because you're now too cold and need to replace your covers. This can go on all...night...long, and deprive you of sleep, causing you to be irritable and fatigued the next day.

The lack of sleep is not the only reason for changes in temperament. Hormone decline causes a drop in two chemicals in the brain that allow you to feel calm and happy. When these two chemicals are gone you can experience mild to severe mood swings, and/or irritability to the point of violence. This can take a toll not only on yourself but your family, friends and associates. One day you're fine, the next day, if anyone even looks at you, you fly into a rage, and the next day all you want to do is cry. Hormonal changes can leave you feeling like Dr. Jekyll and Mrs. Hyde. Many women have told me that they "don't feel like themselves," or that they "don't understand why they have changed so much," or that they "just aren't the same person they used to be."

Your pituitary is like a mom trying to her child to get up in the morning. At first she calls in a normal tone of voice. When they don't get up, she raises her voice a bit, but still no child at the breakfast table. She keeps raising her voice until she's yelling.

This is basically what your pituitary does in your body. When ovarian production is down by, let's say 5%, your pituitary only needs to talk in a normal tone of voice, (send a very small amount of FSH to your ovaries) and this doesn't require any dilation of the blood vessels.

For years this hormonal conversation between your pituitary and ovaries takes place without you being aware of it. But as estradiol production gets lower and lower, your pituitary starts raising its voice. The louder it talks to the ovaries, the wider it dilates the blood vessels, and sooner or later you will start to 'feel' this conversation as hot flashes, as I said, mild at first, but growing in severity over time.

SO WHAT'S A GIRL TO DO?

Replace the missing hormones, but that's not as simple as it sounds. HRT can be deadly if you don't know what you're doing. There's so much you need to know to make sure you're safe when using HRT, but the problem is, that information has not been available to you…until now.

You need to know several things about the HRT industry, such as:

- The truth about 'menopause'.
- The truth about hormone testing.
- The truth about what 'range' you're in.
- The truth about where that range comes from.
- What kind of hormones are available, and which ones are the best to use.
- The truth about how compounding pharmacies make HRT products.
- The truth about estrogen and cancer

What your practitioner 'doesn't' know about the HRT industry.

*Most of this information is available in my booklet called *"The Truth About Hormone Testing"*.

THE DIFFERENT TYPES OF HORMONES

All hormones are not created equal. You need to know what 'kind' of hormones are on the market, and what the effects of using them are, so you can make the correct choice.

Hormones comes in two forms, bioidentical (the *exact* same chemical structure as those made by the human body), and, *non*-bioidentical (hormones with a *different* chemical structure than those made by the human body), and it's that *difference* in chemical structure that causes all the problems. It's the non-bioidentical hormones that cause all the strokes, heart attacks and cancer.

The most commonly prescribes HRT is the non-bioidentical kind called '*equilins*' and '*progestins*'. Equilins are *non*-bioidentical estrogens made by dehydrating the urine of pregnant horses. Progestins are non-bioidentical progesterone. Studies have shown both non-bioidentical equilins and progestins can cause strokes, heart attacks and cancer.

The most commonly prescribed non-bioidentical HRT product made from equilins is called 'Premarine' (its name was derived from these three words: 'pre' - **pregnant +** 'mar' - **mare +** 'in' - **urine**). The most commonly prescribed *non-bioidentical* progestin is called 'Provera'. When these two products are prescribed together it's called PremPro. These non-bioidentical hormones have been on the market since the early 1960's and have caused the most strokes, heart attacks, liver damage, cancer and deaths, of all HRT.

Equilins are dangerous for the following reasons:
- Their chemical structure is that of a female horse, not a female human.
- They're **powerful** blood vessel constrictors and are known to cause fatal heart attacks.
- They clot blood cells causing strokes.
- They're mainly prescribed *without* progesterone which causes the condition of 'estrogen dominance', which is known to cause breast, uterine and ovarian cancer, heart attacks and strokes.
- They're administered orally, which causes liver damage.

Progestins are dangerous for the following reasons:
- They do not have the same *protective* effects as bioidentical progesterone which causes the symptoms of estrogen dominance.
- They clot blood and cause strokes.
- They cause headaches and migraines
- They lower blood sugar causing diabetes

There are quite a few other synthetic estrogens and progestins on the market, so don't assume that just because it doesn't say Premarine or Primpro on the label that it's safe, *or* bioidentical.

Since 2002, over 10,000 law suits have been filed by women who have developed cancer while using Premarin or Primpro. Wyeth, the company that manufactures the drugs, has so far been made to award over $300 million to victims of these drugs, they have only settled about 2,500 of the over 10,000 law suites, and more are being filed every day.

The right thing to do is to use bioidentical estradiol and progesterone, and use it topically. **NEVER** ingest **ANY** hormones. Estradiol and progesterone (as well as other hormones) are secreted *directly* into the blood stream, not into the digestive tract. When you ingest them, your body digests them and the metabolites from digestion are extremely toxic to the liver and can cause liver damage over time.

If you're wondering why your doctor hasn't warned you about the dangers of *non*-bioidentical HRT, it's because the pharmaceutical companies that make Premarin, Provera, all the other *non*-bioidentical HRT, *and* birth control pills, have played down their harmful, and often deadly side effects. Then your doctor downplays them to you, or doesn't tell you about them at all.

Non-bioidentical HRT has been ingrained in the medical profession since the 1960's, and the only way to get rid of them is to educate women to 'just say no' if their doctor tries to prescribe it.

I TRIED BIOIDENTICAL HRT BUT IT DIDN'T WORK!

I've heard this from so many women over the last 19 years of helping them regain hormonal balance, and have found that there are several potential reasons why they didn't have success, and they are:

- The product was made in a compounding pharmacy.
- They were not using enough.
- They needed estradiol, but were only using progesterone.
- They were instructed to use it incorrectly by their practitioner.
- The product was of poor quality.
- The product contained ingredients that prevented a good amount, or all, of the hormones from being absorbed into the blood stream.
- They were taking birth control pills at the same time.
- They were taking anti-depressants or anti-anxiety drugs at the same time.
- The product didn't have any or enough hormones in it.
- The product contained herbal extracts that interfered with hormones.

- They were eating or drinking something that interfered with hormones.
- Or a combination of the above.

NEVER USE HERBS AS HRT

I'm a master herbalist and I can tell you that herbs are great for many things, BUT NOT FOR HORMONE REPLACEMENT!

Hormones are special chemicals that carry specific instructions to specific cells. Each hormone gives different instructions to different cells. All cells have little slots on their surface and inside of them called 'receptors'. These receptors are how the hormones enter the cells. The receptor sites are like locks and the hormones are like keys. The exact, right key (hormone) needs to fit into the exact, right lock (receptor) for the correct instructions to be given to the cell.

There are about 5000 different plants that contain chemicals that are *similar* enough to hormones in structure that they can fit into their receptors (Soy, Wild yam, Dong Qui, Chaste Tree (vitex), Black Cohosh, Blue cohosh, Red Raspberry, Saw Palmetto, Noni, Goji, Asci, Resveratrol, and Ginseng, just to name a few). These chemicals have come to be called 'phytoestrogens'. But there is *no such thing* as phytoestrogen, plants *do not contain* estrogen, progesterone, or *any other hormone*. These plant chemicals are *not* hormones and do *not* do what hormones do.

Ingesting these plants, or their extracts, in an attempt to balance your hormones will not work because your body cannot make them into hormones. That can only be done by a pharmaceutical manufacturer. So don't ever let anyone who you think knows what their talking about, tell you that you can balance your hormones by taking herbs (or any other type of supplement).

There are over 115 different symptoms that can occur during hormone decline, but most women only associate hot flashes and night sweats, and the fact that their period stops with it. Hot flashes are your body's way of saying that there are too many receptor sites without hormones in them. They're your body's way of telling you it needs more hormones.

The chemicals in herbs just fill-up the receptor, and in some cases can stop hot flashes, but that's only because there's 'something' in the receptor. The problem is that your pituitary can't tell the difference between wild yam extract, soy, or an actual hormone, it just knows there's 'something' in the receptor and so it stops asking for hormones (stops hot flashing). If you take herbs and your hot flashes stop, you could think that your hormones are balanced...but that is *far* from the case. Taking herbs that block hormone receptors can actually make things worse. If the cells do not get the right instructions, they do not function properly, things start breaking down, and symptoms eventually appear or get worse.

There are also petrochemicals (made from petroleum) that can fit into your hormone receptors and cause cancer. A petrochemical in plastic is the biggest culprit. That chemical is called Bispheniol A (PBA). This is the most cancer-causing chemical in your environment. It causes birth defects and 5 types of cancer: beast, uterine, prostate, brain and bone (leukemia). See my book *"How My Neighbor Accidentally Cured Her Cancer"* for details.

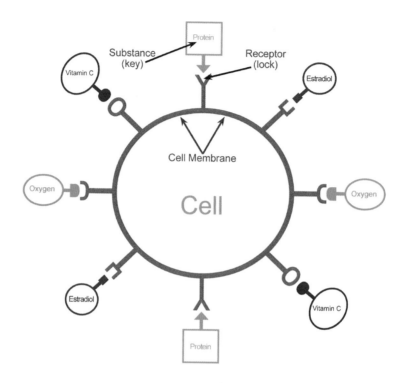

HOW TO STOP THE SYMPTOMS
OF HORMONE DECLINE

There's only one way to stop your symptoms, and that's to halt their decline and bring them back up to their optimum levels, and the only way to do that is HRT. You cannot eat, supplement or exercise your way out of this. You need to replace the exact molecules your body is no longer making but desperately needs, and those molecules are not found in foods, vitamins, minerals or herbs. You need to replace your estradiol, progesterone and testosterone (if needed), and the products you use need to be made of 100% plant derived ingredients...NO PETROCHEMICALS!

Any HRT product you use should *not* contain any of the following ingredients:

- Benzyl alcohol (toxic solvent)
- Methanol (toxic solvent)
- Carbomer (petroleum derivative)
- Polyethylene Glycols, PEGs, Peg Stearates (petroleum derivatives)
- Hyroxyethylcellulose (contains a high degree of lead and heavy metals)
- Mineral oil (toxic - restricts absorption)
- Methylparaben or Propylparaben (toxic preservatives)
- Herbs or herbal extracts (are not hormones and interfere with hormones)
- Soy Isoflavins (are not hormones and interfere with hormones)
- Phytoestrogens (are not hormones and interfere with hormones)
- Gels of any kind (prevent hormones from being absorbed)

Any HRT product you use should contain non-toxic ingredients such as the ones below:

- Oils such as coconut, palm, olive, etc.
- Glycerin (plant derived, helps skin retain moisture)
- Steric Acid (plant derived thickener)
- Emulsifying wax NF (plant derived, holds water and oil together)
- Progesterone (bioidentical only)
- Estrogen (bioidentical only)
- Testosterone (bioidentical only)
- DHEA (bioidentical only)
- Cortisol (bioidentical only)

ARE THERE ANY SIDE EFFECTS
TO USING BIO-IDENTICAL HRT?

The most common 'side effect' of using a quality HRT product, made correctly with non-toxic ingredients and used in the proper way, is relief from your symptoms of hormone decline. Two of my customers reported reducing fibrous tumors in their breasts by 50% in just one week... *no exaggeration!* Others have reported feeling saner, sleeping better, breast swelling going down, anxiety, depression and mood swings vanishing, migraines and severe headaches disappearing, PMS being a thing of the past, sleeping again, and *MUCH MORE!*

There are a few negative things that can happen if you use too much progesterone and/or estradiol. Too much progesterone can cause you to feel like you have morning sickness, and cause your period to be heavier. Too much estradiol and you could experience tender breasts, cramps during ovulation and/or your period, heavier periods, sore breasts, and headaches.

Later in this publication I'll tell you where to go to read the answer to numerous Frequently Asked Questions. that explain the side effect of using too much or too little estradiol and/or progesterone.

BUT DOESN'T ESTROGEN CAUSE CANCER?

Women are always asking me this question and my answer is always "yes, if you use the wrong kind of any of the 3 estrogens, or you use bioidentical estradiol incorrectly". Estradiol is one of the most abundant hormones in your body, and is used by almost every cell. But the main tissues that use it are breast, uterine, cervical, vulvar and nerve, blood vessel and brain, and it has a significant effect on all of them. As long as your hormone cycle is normal, you don't develop cancer. But as soon as you fail to ovulate, use non-bioidentical hormones, or use any HRT incorrectly, you increase your chances of developing cancer.

The fact, is that it's not actually the estradiol or the estrone that causes cancer; it's one of the waste products from breaking them down. The hormones are broken down in a cascade, like a staircase.

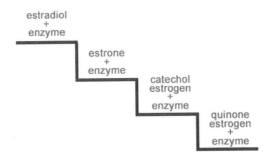

Let's take estradiol for instance, it starts off as estradiol on the top step, then an enzyme converts it to estrone on the second step, then a different enzyme converts it to catechol (a reduced form of estrone) estrogen on the third step, and on the fourth step it's converted to two different quinone (another reduced form of estrone) estrogens. One of them is perfectly harmless, but the other one can get back into the cell and damage the parts of the cells that allow it to fix the damage, or self-destruct if the damage is too great. Simply put, if these two parts of the cell are damaged, the cell will keep reproducing, and at that point it is considered cancer. See my e-book, "*How My Neighbor Accidentally Cured Her Cancer*" for full details of how cancer starts, and what additional chemicals in your environment can cause it. A *MUST* read for anyone breathing.

The enzyme that converts catechol estrogen into quinone estrogen is called Aromatase and is made by your fat cells. The more fat cells you have, the more Aromatase you make, and the more catechol estrogen is converted into quinone estrogen. This is why overweight and obese women have a greater incidence of cancer.

Now, when I say "...if you don't use it correctly", I mean that using *any* estrogen, *non*-bioidentical or bioidentical, without using progesterone along with it, almost *doubles* the amount of quinone estrogen in your system, which almost doubles your chances of developing cancer. Women who have had their uterus removed are generally not prescribed progesterone along with estrogen. They're told that progesterone's only function is to protect the uterus, and since they no longer have one, they don't need it... **WRONG, WRONG WRONG!!!!!!!!!!!!!!**

Practitioners also tell women that bioidentical estrogen is safe, that it doesn't cause cancer because it's bioidentical... ***WRONG AGAIN!*** You can develop cancer from the estradiol your own body makes just as soon as you stop ovulating. That's the real bioidentical estrogen, so logic should tell you that you can develop cancer from the use of bioidentical *HRT* as well. It's ***totally*** unethical for practitioners to mislead women on a matter that's vital to their very lives, either by ignorance or through greed.

But, there are things you can do to protect yourself from developing cancer, and if you did develop it (by whatever means), you can easily kill it. There is a natural plant extract that can stop Armoatase from turning quinone estrogen into a powerful cancer cancer-causing agent.

There's a product that contains plant chemicals that starve cancer cells to death, and tells them to kill themselves. See my e-book, "***How My Neighbor Accidentally Cured Her Cancer***" for full details.

HOW DO I KNOW IF I NEED HRT?

First of all, every woman will stop ovulating at some point and need to begin by using bioidentical progesterone. You should suspect that you need to start using progesterone if you experience any of the symptoms listed at the beginning of this publication, or as soon as you start to see changes in your periods.

Your menstrual cycle is supposed to be 28 days long. When it gets shorter than that, and your periods get heavier, it tells you that you're skipping ovulation and becoming estrogen dominant. If you start getting occasional headaches, start putting on weight that will not come off easily, find that movies make you cry easier, or that little things bother you more than they used to, if you find yourself saying, "Is it hot in here or is it just me?", or if now you consider yourself a light sleeper, your hair is starting to thin or you notice more hair in your brush than usual, you're becoming estrogen dominant. If your sex drive and your memory just aren't what they used to be, or you're craving sweets (especially chocolate) more than usual, you're becoming estrogen dominant and you need to start using bioidentical progesterone.

If you've replaced your progesterone but you're still having hot flashes, vaginal dryness and/or irritation, you can't sleep and your periods are getting lighter, farther in between, or you're beginning to skip them, you're now experiencing symptoms of low estrogen and need to replace it as well. Progesterone only relieves the symptoms of progesterone deficiency, so if your symptoms are coming from low estradiol, you must replace it too before all your symptoms will be relieved.

I found that when I first started having hot flashes, I would feel normal one minute and then get hot the next. I used progesterone alone and it stopped that for about eight months. Then, something changed, I just felt hot all the time, as if I had a fever, then I would have a hot flash on top of that! No amount of progesterone changed that. It took me a few weeks to figure out what was going on, order some estradiol and make a new cream. I put it on and in about twenty minutes my body temperature felt normal again, the hot flashes stopped, and that night I slept seven straight hours.

IN CONCLUSION

Being in the HRT industry for 19 years has allowed me to learn all the ins and outs of it, and all its dirty little secrets. My intention in writing this booklet is to educate women about hormone decline, the problems that come with it, and to make women aware of the unethical practices in the industry.

Replacing your declining hormones can be safe and easy if you know what 'to' and 'not' to do. Over the years I've developed a protocol (Definition: protocol - a plan for a medical treatment) of using HRT in a way that will stop the decline of your hormones, bring them back to their optimum levels, and do it in a way that (I'm not allowed to say, 'keeps you safe', so I'll just say, that greatly reduces the risks that accompany doing so. It will also teach you how to kill and prevent cancer with simple plant materials, so that if you (or anyone you know) does happen to develop cancer.

I hope this information has been helpful to you. If it has, please pass it on to your friends and family, as they may need it as much, or even more, than you.

Thank you for reading this publication,
Sindi Holmlund

Researcher, writer, herbalist, developer and manufacturer of chemical free health and beauty products, owner of Accurate Diagnostic Services laboratory and Right Way compounding pharmacy.

If you would like help with the issues in this publication e-mail me at: sindih@bonvida.biz